He's Got My Number

He's Got My Number
(and Other Sketches)

A Lillenas Drama Resource

By STEPHEN HICKS
& JERRY COHAGAN

Lillenas Publishing Co.
Kansas City, MO 64141

Cover design by Jeff Lane
Cover photo by Russ Hansen

Dedication

For our parents,
Chester and Beverly Cohagan
and
Elvin and Lois Hicks,
who have never once asked
why we didn't get a real job.

Contents

Preface

The preface of a book is usually a good place for the authors to explain the trials of finally getting a book published. How we have slaved over the manuscripts for years; been turned down by dozens of publishers; rejected by even more editors. How we have overcome insurmountable obstacles in order to make these scripts available to the public.

Basically, however, we threw this material together in an afternoon. Then held the publisher's poodle hostage to get it printed. That's probably not the usual procedure for getting a book published. But then there isn't much about this book that is "usual." This book contains some of the material we have used as "Hicks & Cohagan, performers of comedy and drama with a Christian perspective."

Since the time we began performing several years ago, we have had thousands of people from across this great land of ours come to us asking for copies of our sketches. Well, maybe not thousands . . . perhaps only a few hundred . . . okay, maybe we've had 17 people mention something to us. But, then, we have always considered ourselves specialists. So for those 17 people and anyone else reading this, we should mention a couple of common threads running through our material.

A quick glance at the book will tell you we have a very casual, informal performance attitude. This is evident by the minimal use of props and set pieces. Oftentimes we will rely simply on a folding chair, a hand prop or two, or the pantomime necessary to establish a door, a television set, or whatever.

You will also discover we do not share many secrets about the art of great acting. Probably because we do not have many secrets about great acting. Or, as some might suggest, we don't know that much about great acting. We do have a couple of areas we try to concentrate on as actors. It is important to remember that tempo and pacing are keys to the success of any performance, especially with a sketch format. It is crucial to keep the story and dialogue moving.

We also try to concentrate on reacting as well as acting. In other words, much of the work an actor does on stage involves more than just speaking lines. An actor must respond and react to the words and actions of others. If you, the actor, appear to be interested in what is happening on stage, then the audience (hopefully) will be interested, too. We have found after years of experience that it is a much more rewarding experience for everyone if the audience is interested and awake. This is perhaps the most basic goal of a performer: Keep the audience conscious.

We have not attempted to apologize or justify using comedy and drama in a spiritual setting. Our belief is that anything that brings us closer to God and His relationship with us is worthy of our consideration and use. Let's hope that whatever medium we may use, those around us will see more of Christ and His love in our lives.

Enjoy and may God bless and use you!

Stephen Hicks and Jerry Cohagan

Acknowledgments

We would like to thank Jennifer Hoyle, Judy Askren, and Mark Boden-stab for the early years when we were known as "The Troupe." (Clever, huh?)

Also, we would like to thank (in lieu of sending him a check) Ed Drake for "The New Christian," which is 99 percent his. (He's a lawyer now, so he doesn't need the money.)

And also Paul Miller for his belief in what we do. (The guy is so gullible.)

And, of course, all the little people.

Other than that, we plead guilty and assume full responsibility for what follows.

THE SKETCHES IN THIS BOOK have been performed in almost every situation imaginable. That is mainly because we love to perform, and as long as the two of us didn't outnumber the audience, we would give it a shot. From church services, youth functions, laymen's retreats, banquets, revivals, seminars, and workshops—to amusement parks, street corners, shopping malls, apartments, and gymnasiums—we have tried and tested these sketches. Their use is limited only by the scope of one's imagination.

They can be used in conjunction with a sermon; as a scripture illustration; or as a part of an evening's entertainment for the church community. They can be used along with special music, or as discussion starters in Sunday Schools or Bible studies.

Whether you use this book to enhance your resource materials or to line the bottom of your pet bird cage, the main asset of these sketches is their adaptability. Always feel free to adapt or edit these sketches to the setting, so that they work for you. They are tools which we hope you will use not only to entertain, but to minister to your community as well.

Mustard Seed Faith

Purpose:

Sometimes it is easier to talk about having faith in God than it is to actually exercise that faith. God says that no matter what the situation is, if we trust Him, He will honor our faithfulness.

Running Time:

3 minutes

Cast:

JERRY. This "mountain climber" is just an average guy looking for a little excitement in life. Little does he know . . .

VOICE (offstage). Here is a "divine" speaking part. The voice can sound like any one of us, male or, yes, even female.

Props:

None

Application:

This sketch is fun for just about anyone to do. It is a simple, easy-to-stage script with a meaningful message. The major challenges concern the part of the mountain climber. Of course, the character should be called by the name of the actor playing the part. The actor must be willing to take the time and effort to establish the setting with at least some use of the pantomimed action. This is a broad, humorous sketch, so feel free to employ your own sound effects. Use lots of facial expression and don't be afraid to give a look of reaction that might be funnier than the actual line of dialogue. Also, remember to continue "holding onto the rope" throughout the entire sketch.

The voice of God should be warm, friendly, and a little fatherly. It should be a voice full of life. Don't worry that it doesn't sound like God. He doesn't always speak in a deep voice with gobs of sound system reverberation.

As with any of our sketches, pace and timing are important. Keep the sketch moving, but at the same time, slow down enough to have fun with it.

❧ ❦

(JERRY *walks on stage with an imaginary rope over his shoulder, looks up at the mountain he is about to scale, which should be placed directly out over the audience. He lays down the rope and begins swinging the end of it back and forth. He throws it up toward the mountaintop and watches it go up and then fall back down, missing the mountain. He gathers the rope back in, muttering to himself, then repeats the process, this time with success. Pulling on the rope a few times to make sure it is secure, he wraps it around his waist, then his leg.)*

JERRY: Okay, baby . . . up we go! *(Begins to pantomime climbing the mountain by pulling himself up by the rope hand over hand. Suddenly he slips and spins around, holding onto the rope with both hands over his head, dangling.)* Help! Help! Somebody help me!

VOICE: Yes, Jerry?

JERRY *(looks around, grins sheepishly):* Who said that?

VOICE: Why, it is I, Jerry.

JERRY: Who's I? *(looking around frantically)* Where's I?

VOICE: Why, I am all around you, Jerry.

JERRY *(slowly as it sinks in):* You mean . . . are You trying to tell me . . . are You . . . *(reverently)* who I think You are?

VOICE: That's right, Jerry.

JERRY *(plays to the voice as if it were out above the audience, greatly relieved):* Boy, am I glad You're here! You see, I was just climbing this stupid mountain when I—

VOICE *(cutting in):* I made that mountain, Jerry.

JERRY (broad smile): Lovely mountain! I love mountains, Lord!

VOICE: Thank you.

JERRY (under his breath with a tinge of sarcasm): You're welcome.

VOICE (quickly): Don't push it, Bucko.

JERRY (sheepishly): I'm sorry, Lord. Anyway, I was climbing this lovely mountain here, when all of the sudden I started to slip. Luckily, I grabbed onto this rope. If anyone can get me out of this, You can. Right, Lord?

VOICE: That's right, Jerry.

JERRY (desperately): Then get me out of it.

VOICE: All right, Jerry. Do you trust Me?

JERRY: Oh, I trust You with all my heart.

VOICE: But do you trust Me with your life?

JERRY (looks below him—beat. Then): Of course I do, Lord. I've got no choice!

VOICE: Do you have faith in Me, Jerry?

JERRY (looking around below him): Do I have faith in You? This is really a bad time for a quiz, Lord—ahh, Yes. Yes, I have faith in You! You get me out of this one and I'll do anything, Lord. I'll be a missionary. I'll go to Africa, the Bahamas—anywhere, Lord! (As an afterthought) I'll even tithe 10 percent.

VOICE: Okay, Jerry. Are you ready?

JERRY (looking up): Oh, I'm ready.

VOICE: Here's what I want you to do, then.

JERRY: Okay . . .

VOICE (beat): Let go of that rope.

JERRY (slowly looks down, starts chuckling, then looks back up): Let go of the rope. That's a funny one, Lord. (Laughs.) A lot of people think You don't have a sense of humor, but I knew You did. (Laughing harder.) Let go of the rope . . . (Abruptly stops laughing—deadpan.) No way.

VOICE: But you said you trusted Me.

JERRY: Well, I do, Lord, but I'm not stupid . . . (grimaces, expecting a lightning bolt).

VOICE: But you said you had faith in Me.

JERRY *(embarrassed)*: Well, I do, Lord, but it only goes so far . . .

VOICE *(disheartened)*: Oh, Jerry . . .

JERRY *(gets an idea, slowly)*: Hey, Lord?

VOICE *(hopeful)*: Yes, Jerry?

JERRY *(looking above)*: Is there anybody else up there I can talk to?

(Blackout)

The Examination

Purpose:

If we call ourselves followers of Jesus, then our words and actions must be patterned after His life. Sometimes it is important to stop for a moment and examine our motives. Does our perspective and response to situations we encounter reflect what Christ would have us say and do?

Running Time:

9-11 minutes

Cast:

DR. PATNODE. A doctor who examines Christian perspectives. He has an irritating ability to get to the nitty-gritty of any situation.

FLOYD LANGLY. An average guy who is sincere, yet somewhat belligerent. He is not always able to grasp the full implications of his attitudes and circumstances.

Props:

1 folding chair
1 white doctor's smock
1 notebook, note pad, or folder
1 pen for the doctor
1 pair of eyeglasses, which the doctor wears

Application:

This sketch is a clever, thought-provoking piece with a sandbag ending. What more could you want? Both characters are a little less flamboyant than our usual type of characters. The moments of zaniness are still there, but the broad physical humor is less evident. That presents a challenge to the actors to establish strong characters who use more subtle nuances of humor. It should be noted that the end of this sketch is not intended to be humorous. It is intended to catch the audience by surprise (like a sandbag falling).

As actors, take the time to let that final moment sink in. Be aware that the sketch is moving towards that moment. Let it build accordingly. But be careful not to tip your hand. As an actor, work for a blend of foreshadowing; but as the characters, let it be surprise.

Along with its humor, this script can have a real moment of impact. And that's the purpose or goal you should work toward: to shake up the audience a little.

❧ ❦ ❧

(One chair center stage: DR. PATNODE is sitting in the chair with his nose buried in a folder. He has glasses on the end of his nose and is humming "Send in the Clowns." When he reaches that particular phrase, "Send in the clowns," he sings it out loud. Immediately the doorbell rings and he completes the phrase by singing, "Don't bother, they're here." Doorbell rings again.)

PATNODE: Coming! Coming . . . just a minute. *(Puts down folder and goes toward imaginary door stage right, where FLOYD LANGLY has been standing ringing the doorbell.)* Who is it?

LANGLY: It's Floyd, Floyd Langly . . . *(straightens his tie).*

PATNODE *(mumbles to himself as he opens door):* . . . Langly, Langly . . . ?

LANGLY *(as PATNODE opens door):* Dr. Patnode! It's good to see you again! *(Grabs his hand.)*

PATNODE *(having his hand pumped):* It's good to see you, too.

LANGLY: Well, I hope I'm not too early. *(Stops shaking hand.)*

PATNODE: No! No, not at all . . . *(Looks puzzled.)* For what?

LANGLY *(taken aback):* We had an appointment . . . to get my Christian perspective examined. *(Looking at his watch.)* 9:30?

PATNODE *(suddenly remembering):* Oh! Yes, of course. *(Looks at LANGLY'S watch.)* Right on time.

LANGLY *(proudly):* Well, I like to be prompt.

PATNODE: And I like to see promptness in a person! *(Both laugh heartily.)* Well, please come in. *(Picking up folder.)* Sorry about the mess. Please, have a seat. *(Gestures to chair.)*

LANGLY *(points to it):* This one here?

PATNODE *(glances around empty room):* Yes, that one there. (LANGLY *sits.*) I'll be honest with you, Mr. Langly. I completely forgot about your appointment.

LANGLY: Wait a minute, Dr. Patnode. I thought you said this was your profession.

PATNODE: Oh, it is my profession, but it seems these days people just don't think they need their Christian perspectives examined very often. I will go for weeks, even months, without ever examining a Christian perspective. Sometimes it's a lonely, lonely job . . . *(Rests his hand on* LANGLY'S *shoulder and stares out into space.)* Kind of like being a Maytag repairman. (LANGLY *follows his gaze off into the land of the brave but sees nothing.)* Well! Enough about me. Ramble, ramble . . . It's YOU we're here to examine. *(Opens up folder.)* Oh, your file is right on top. Well. It's been a while, hasn't it?

LANGLY: Well, yes—it has.

PATNODE: I'm going to have to ask you a few questions, kind of update the file.

LANGLY *(generously):* You can ask me anything. I don't have anything to hide. *(Smiles broadly.)*

PATNODE *(smiles back):* I hope not. I see here according to our records you were saved in 1972?

LANGLY *(proudly):* April 22, 1972! *(Leans toward* PATNODE, *confiding.)* I can even remember the very hour.

PATNODE: Precious, just precious. *(Jotting in file)* Now, at that time you had perfect vision?

LANGLY: Twenty-twenty, straight as an arrow.

PATNODE *(continuing to survey the file):* Now we didn't see you again until four years later. At that time you came in complaining about a little blurred focus?

LANGLY: Let me just level with you, Doctor. That was my first year on our church board and we had a big stink that year. I mean a big stink. We were split right down the middle on the church budget. We couldn't decide whether to get a new sound system for the choir, which I might add they desperately needed, or to get luminescent praying hands for the Communion table.

PATNODE (*looks up from file*): Well . . . what did you decide?

LANGLY: We got one speaker and one luminescent praying hand. Big stink, Doctor, big stink.

PATNODE (*resumes writing*): Wisdom of Solomon. Now. At that time we fitted you for some lenses, correct?

LANGLY: That is correct, yes.

PATNODE (*noting in file*): You chose contacts?

LANGLY (*slightly embarrassed*): Well, yes—I did.

PATNODE (*looks up from file, simply*): Why?

LANGLY (*uncomfortable pause; then rises and paces around the room a bit*): Well, like I said, that was my first year on the church board and . . . well, no one else on the church board wore glasses. So I just assumed their Christian perspectives were normal. In fact, no one else in the church wore glasses and I didn't want them to think that perhaps I needed a little help . . . you know, a little guidance. And of course with contact lenses you couldn't tell. (*Sits back down, trying to dismiss it.*) Like I said, Doctor, it was my first year. Just a vanity problem with me back then. (*Crosses his arms and stares out in front of him.*)

PATNODE: Do you still wear contacts?

LANGLY (*beat, softly*): Yes, I do . . .

PATNODE (*writing*): I see. Well, we really ought to run a couple tests here. To keep all the information up to date.

LANGLY: That's fine with me.

PATNODE (*standing at his side*): All right, then, let's start with the eye chart. (*Points at it directly in front of* LANGLY *out over the audience.*)

LANGLY (*staring straight out*): Sounds good to me; where is it?

PATNODE: It's right there (*pointing*), directly in front of you.

LANGLY (*focuses in*): Oh, there it is. I can see the big *E* (*squinting*). Wait a minute, that could be a *B*. No! That's an *E*.

PATNODE: It's an *E*, I assure you. Each one of those rows of letters spells out a word. They get progressively smaller each row. I'm going to spell out the row and you tell me what word I spell out.

LANGLY: I can do this.

PATNODE: Let's hope so. Let's start with the big word right at the top: *P-E-O-P-L-E.*

LANGLY: People. *(Simply)* You and I are people, everybody's people. Even I know that.

PATNODE: That's very astute of you. Must be a college graduate?

LANGLY: No, but I went six years . . .

PATNODE: The word right below that: *C-H-U-R-C-H.*

LANGLY *(beat)*: Church. *(Sees a glimmer of light.)* The Church is made up of people! Each word kind of relates to the one before, doesn't it?

PATNODE: That's right. (LANGLY *giggles at his own brilliance.* PATNODE *eyes him cautiously)* Wonderful . . . let's try the one below that: *P-A-S-T-O-R.*

LANGLY *(thinks it through)*: *P-A-S,* that's pas. *T-O-R,* that's tor. *(Putting it together)* Pastor, Pastor! The pastor is the leader of the church, which is made up of people. This is kind of like a pyramid; this is like being on one of those game shows!

PATNODE *(tongue in cheek)*: Only you're not going to win $25,000! (LANGLY *laughs heartily.* PATNODE *chuckles weakly.)* A little doctor humor, there . . .

LANGLY *(stops laughing abruptly, stares at chart)*: Very little.

PATNODE: Moving on: *P-R-O-T-E-S-T-A-N-T.* (LANGLY *squints, then looks at* PATNODE *sheepishly; he obliges by repeating it)* *P-R-O-T-E-S-T-A-N-T.*

LANGLY *(attempts to sound it out)*: Pro . . . pro . . . *(looks at* PATNODE *for help)*

PATNODE *(reluctantly helps)*: Pro . . . protest . . .

LANGLY: Pro . . . protest . . . *(a sudden revelation)* Protestant! *(Emphasis is on second syllable.)* A mob rioter! He starts riots in churches!

PATNODE *(rubbing his own head)*: No, no. *(Correcting him)* Protestant. (LANGLY *stares at him stupidly.)* Your church is part of the Protestant movement.

LANGLY: Oh, you're talking Communism—

PATNODE *(attempts to explain)*: No, no, I don't think I am. Your church is part of the denominations that make up the Protestant movement.

LANGLY (indignant): Well, I never read about Protestant in the Bible, I'll tell you that. Denominations throw me off. (Dismisses it.)

PATNODE: Let's move on then; J-O-H-N-T-H-E-B-A-P-T-I-S-T. (LANGLY pulls at the corners of his eyelids) J-O-H-N-T-H-E-B-A-P-T-I-S-T.

LANGLY (sounding it out as if it's one long French word): Jeantheebyaah, Jeantheeboo—

PATNODE: No, no. It's English.

LANGLY (not listening): Jeantheeboobaa, it's French, isn't it?

PATNODE: No, it's English. It's three English words.

LANGLY: Three words? You're trying to trick me.

PATNODE: No, I'm not! It's three English words!

LANGLY: Give me some hints, hints . . .

PATNODE: Hints . . . ? Ahh, a New Testament character.

LANGLY (sarcastic): Well, that narrows it right down.

PATNODE (desperately trying to help): Ah, big into animal skins!

LANGLY (getting more excited with each clue): New Testament, into animal skins. Oh, I know this—

PATNODE (getting caught up in it): Big into water—

LANGLY: Ahh, into water!

PATNODE: Prophesied the coming of the Messiah!

LANGLY (continuing to build with excitement): The Messiah! John! John Handel! (Jumping up and exploding) Handel's Messiah! (Turns triumphantly to PATNODE.)

PATNODE (stares in silence): No . . . no. It's John the Baptist.

LANGLY: Oh, I've read about him in the Book of Collisions.

PATNODE: Book of what?

LANGLY (sitting down): Listen, buddy, I know my scriptures. The French language threw me off.

PATNODE: Fine, fine. Let's try one more.

LANGLY (looking at chart): That's awfully small print.

PATNODE: Give it a shot. C-O-R-N-E-R-S-T-O-N-E.

LANGLY (*scoots forward on chair*): Hints, I need more hints . . .

PATNODE: Another name for the Messiah?

LANGLY (*thinking*): . . . another name . . .

PATNODE: The basis of our faith . . .

LANGLY: I ought to know this.

PATNODE: It's what we build all our beliefs on.

LANGLY (*feigned enthusiasm*): It's on the tip of my tongue.

PATNODE: The foundation of our beliefs; we build on this . . . the basis
 . . . of . . . (LANGLY *is staring stupidly in front of him.* PATNODE *sighs.*)
 Okay, Mr. Langly. I think I've seen enough.

LANGLY: I bet very few Christians get that word.

PATNODE (*almost to himself*): Not near as many as used to. (*Begins to ad-
just an imaginary eye machine in front of* LANGLY's *eyes.*) Let's just
 have a look through the refractor here. You're not scared of this, are
 you?

LANGLY: Not at all. (PATNODE *finishes adjusting it and steps behind*
 LANGLY.) Wait a minute (*frightened*), I can't see anything.

PATNODE: That's because I've got the protective caps over the lenses.

LANGLY (*relieved, he reaches to remove them*): Oh, thank goodness. Let's
 get those off of there—

PATNODE (*slaps his wrist*): DON'T TOUCH! Cost me $10,000. I'm still
 paying on it.

LANGLY (*rubbing his wrist*): That explains your fees.

PATNODE (*sighs*): I'm going to give you a choice between two lenses and
 you tell me which one you prefer.

LANGLY: I can certainly do this. (*Looks in machine, face front.*)

PATNODE (*stands behind* LANGLY *and flips imaginary lenses over one eye and
 then the other*): No. 1, concern for others. No. 2, concern for yourself.

LANGLY: No. 1. Concern for others. Every Christian ought to know that.

PATNODE: All right. No. 1, a steak dinner for you and your family. No. 2,
 send food to the starving people of Cambodia.

LANGLY: No. 2, send the starving people to Cambia.

PATNODE: No. That's send *food* to the starving people of *Cambodia.*

LANGLY: Oh, sure, let's do that. That's much more important than a steak dinner for me and my family.

PATNODE: All right, let's try this one. No. 1, a garage sale for you and your neighborhood. No. 2, send used clothes, toys, and other items to the people of Ethiopia.

LANGLY *(thinking out loud):* Garage sale would sure be nice, extra income . . . *(Looks at* PATNODE *for support.)* I could tithe more that week, you know. (PATNODE *is noncommittal,* LANGLY *grumbles to himself.)* All right, No. 2. Give 'em to the crazy Ethiopes.

PATNODE: Wonderful spirit. Let's go back to this one: concern for others, or concern for yourself.

LANGLY *(begrudgingly):* No. 1, concern for others.

PATNODE: Just a couple more. No. 1, attend a weekly Bible study. No. 2, watch Monday Night Football.

LANGLY: Can I see those again?

PATNODE: Sure, No. 1, attend a weekly Bible study; No. 2, watch Monday Night Football.

LANGLY: No. 2—Monday Night Football is clear as a bell!

PATNODE: Clear as a bell . . .

LANGLY: Besides, Bible studies aren't one of my gifts.

PATNODE: Ah. Let's try this one—No. 1, a weekend ski trip in the Rockies; No. 2, invest time and money in local church ministry. (LANGLY *slumps in his chair.)* No. 1, a weekend ski trip in the Rockies; No. 2, invest time and money in a local church ministry.

LANGLY *(glancing shyly at* PATNODE): You ski . . . ?

PATNODE: Well, no, I don't.

LANGLY: You ever been to the Rockies . . . ?

PATNODE: No, I haven't.

LANGLY: Oh, it's beautiful up there *(inspiration coming)* . . . God's country! That's what it is, God's country! You know, I work pretty hard and sometimes it would be good for me to get away. Kind of have a . . . a mountaintop experience with the Lord up there in the Rockies. He could revive me up there. Then I'd feel like getting involved in my local church. Then I'd feel like giving my time and energies, and . . . and . . . I, ahh . . . *(swallows)* I pretty much want to go to the Rockies.

PATNODE (*softly*): Let's try this again—No. 1, concern for others; No. 2, concern for yourself. (LANGLY *starts to respond but stops, slowly looking down at his hands, avoiding the choice.*) No. 1, concern for others; No. 2, concern for yourself . . . (*no response*). No. 1, concern for others . . . (PATNODE's *voice trails off, moves imaginary machine*) Well, Mr. Langly, I think I have a pretty clear picture of your Christian perspective. (*Looks at folder.*) I think I can safely say that your Christian perspective is perfectly normal.

LANGLY (*stands up, obviously relieved, and starts to leave*): Oh, good!

PATNODE: Mr. Langly, (LANGLY *stops.*) You're totally blind. (LANGLY *turns and meets* PATNODE's *gaze, stunned.*)

(*Blackout*)

The New Christian

Purpose:

It seems that everyone has a different key to being a successful Christian. It's easy to figure out that if we just get that one area right, we will be successful. But about that time, someone else comes along and tells us that the real key to success is something completely different. All of this can be confusing, especially to a new Christian. After all, Jesus said that we should pattern ourselves after Him, not after those around us.

Running time:

5-7 minutes

Cast:

NEW CHRISTIAN
PROUD CHARACTER
CONCERNED CHARACTER
HAPPY CHARACTER
BURDENED CHARACTER
SUBTLE CHARACTER
AVERAGE CHARACTER

(All characters may be played by one actor or as many as six actors.)

Props:

One sign with the word "Christian" printed on one side, and the word "Help!" on the other side. It should be large enough to be read from the audience (about 16" x 24"). There should be a string attached so that it can hang around the neck of NEW CHRISTIAN.
1 Bible, preferably hardbound

1 sporty-looking cap, the kind people wear when driving their European sports cars
1 limp hat, suitable for wringing
1 silly-looking hat, Mickey Mouse ears, or Disneyland cap
1 construction helmet, also known as hard hat
1 pair of very "hip" or "new wave" sunglasses
1 small black book or note pad to serve as a miniature Bible; should fit in shirt pocket

Application:

This sketch is one of the more popular ones, partially, at least, because it allows for farcical humor. And it lets us laugh at ourselves and others without feeling mean or vicious. It is satire with a soft edge. The script offers some interesting challenges for the performers involved. As the new Christian, you are faced with the demand of conveying the entire character without words. It means utilizing your entire body and face for expressions. The more vivid and expansive your reactions are, the better. For the person or persons portraying the rest of the characters, it is important to clearly differentiate between each one. Along with using different hats and props, consider using different voices and body mannerisms. These characters are really caricatures. They are exaggerated composites of the people around us. With the blend of these outlandish characters and pantomime it should provide an interesting time for the performers and the audience.

(NEW CHRISTIAN *walks on stage wearing a sign around his neck which says "Christian" in big letters. He is carrying a "Living Bible" and grinning widely. He stops center stage and looks around very innocently.)*

PROUD CHARACTER *(enters wearing sporty cap, struts by* NEW CHRISTIAN, *abruptly stops and notices sign):* Christian? (CHRISTIAN *nods yes.)* New Christian? *(Rather sheepishly nods again.)* I could tell. Listen, let me just share with you what I've discovered in my own successful, and I might add, dynamic Christian life-style. And that is that we Christians have got to look, act, and be—proud. (CHRISTIAN *looks slightly shocked.)* After all, we have something the rest of the world doesn't have! You get a new sports car, you wheel that baby out there so everybody can see what they don't have. We gotta do the same thing. Can you look proud for me? (CHRISTIAN *shrugs.)* Can you get those shoulders up and stick out that chest . . . (CHRISTIAN *does so, only his eyes are crossed.)* Listen, in this day and age of Clark Kents, we have got to dare to be—Supermen! *(Both strike a Superman pose, with hands on hips gazing into the great blue yonder.* PROUD CHARACTER *steps back and looks him up and down.)* Not bad, for a beginner. *(*PROUD CHARACTER *struts on off.* CHRISTIAN *continues to hold pose.)*

CONCERNED CHARACTER *(enters sniveling and wringing at hat between his hands, bumps into Christian's chest):* Christian, huh? *(*CHRISTIAN *nods head arrogantly.)* You know, I've discovered in my joyful walk with the Lord that more important than being proud is being concerned. *(Continues to snivel throughout the whole speech.)* After all, there's a whole world out there that's dying and going straight to . . . well, you know where they're going. And we have to let them know that we are meek, humble, caring, nonviolent individuals. *(Looks at* CHRISTIAN *and swiftly smacks him in the chest.)* Get that chest in! *(*CHRISTIAN *does so immediately, surprised.)* I mean *(sniveling)* could you get that chest in, please? Thank you. Can you look concerned for me? Kind of slope your shoulders and tilt your head to the left. *(*CHRISTIAN *does so, except he tilts his head to the right.)* I said left! *(*CHRISTIAN *quickly corrects himself.)* Thank you. Now can you give me a lower lip quiver of concern? *(Both quiver their lower lips.)* And how about a tear; can you give me a tear? *(*CHRISTIAN *tries to squeeze out a tear, but can't)* . . . That's okay. It took me several years to work up to the tear. Say, it's been a real joy helping a fellow believer along the way. *(Snivels on offstage.* CHRISTIAN *continues to quiver his lip and generally look in pain.)*

HAPPY CHARACTER *(comes skipping across stage wearing a beanie or Mickey Mouse ears):* Hi! *(*CHRISTIAN *gives him a weak wave.)* What's the matter, you look like you've been run through a blender. Come on! We Christians are happy, happy, happy! All the time! Happy, happy, happy, happy! Someone comes along and runs over our puppy, we smile. *(*HAPPY CHARACTER *gives a cheesy grin.)* Someone steals our new microwave, we smile. *(Repeats his grin.)* Because we Christians are happy all the time! Can you look happy for me? Kinda get those shoulders up a little and give me a smile . . . *(*CHRISTIAN *grins sheepishly.)* Show me some teeth! *(*CHRISTIAN *smiles for all he's worth.)* Oh, goody! How about some big eyes? *(*CHRISTIAN *opens his eyes wide.)* And a joyful bounce, can you do this? *(Both bounce.)* Oh, great! How about a one-way sign? Oh, goody gumdrops! Bye-bye. Have a nice day, PTL! *(Goes bouncing offstage.* CHRISTIAN *continues to bounce, only circles his ear with his finger, indicating that "Happy" is a loony tune, then quickly raises arm again with one-way sign.)*

BURDENED CHARACTER *(enters wearing a hard hat and looking mean, crosses in front of bouncing* CHRISTIAN *who swiftly slaps* BURDENED CHARACTER *on top of hard hat and smiles broadly.* BURDENED CHARACTER *grabs his head in pain and spins around):* What do you think you are doing? (CHRISTIAN *shrugs.*) Cut out that hopping! *(Physically stops him from hopping.)* Put that arm down! *(Puts his arm down for him.)* And wipe that silly smirk off your face! (CHRISTIAN *drops smile quickly.*) We Christians can't be hopping around grinning all the time, not when there are responsibilities and burdens to bear. No, sir. I wasn't in the church three months before I got my responsibility, my burden to bear. *(Drills his forefinger into* CHRISTIAN'S *chest.)* Who do you think it is that cleans those filthy, vile, disgusting church bathrooms? I do! And it's a joy *(grinding his teeth).* It's a privilege to serve *(growls).* I'm happy to do it. What about you? Can you look like you're shouldering some burdens, kind of scrunch up those shoulders with the weight of the world on 'em and suck in that chest . . . *(They both do so.)* And turn the corners of your mouth down and pierce your eyebrows together so people can see what a joy it is to serve the Lord. (CHRISTIAN *does so.*) There, that's better! I'll see *you* in the church bathrooms. *(Stomps off;* CHRISTIAN *continues to glare out and work at looking mean.)*

SUBTLE CHARACTER *(comes slinking on stage walking backwards to make sure he isn't being followed. He is wearing mirror sunglasses and bumps into mean* CHRISTIAN. SUBTLE CHARACTER *spins around, frightened, spots sign around* CHRISTIAN'S *neck and quickly covers it with his arms. Almost whispering):* What do you think you are doing? People are gonna know you're a Christian with that sign on! (CHRISTIAN *looks totally confused.*) In this day and age, you can't afford to turn people off. You have got to mix in. You have got to . . . *(adjusts his sunglasses)* identify. You can't be a neon sign flashing "Christian, Christian, Christian." No, you got to flash *(under his breath)* "Suble, subtle, subtle." That sign has got to go. (CHRISTIAN *looks shocked.*) Got . . . to . . . go . . . (CHRISTIAN *reluctantly takes off sign and drops it on the floor.*) That's better. And how many Christians do you still see carrying those big Bibles? That's going to make a negative impression. It has got to go, too. *(Takes Bible from* CHRISTIAN *and pulls out of his pocket a small black pad.)* If you gotta carry scripture around, carry something a little smaller. *(Gives black book to* CHRISTIAN.*)* That's an edited version, just the important verses in it. (CHRISTIAN *sticks it in his pocket.*) There! Now you look like the rest of us. (CHRISTIAN *looks out at audience, very dejected.*) What do you look so confused about? *(Before* CHRISTIAN *can respond,* SUBTLE CHARACTER *slinks on offstage.* CHRISTIAN CHARACTER *looks around himself, totally confused; then looks at sign on floor, throws his arms up in a gesture of "Forget it!" He crosses his arms in dejection.)*

NONDESCRIPT CHARACTER *(enters whistling to himself, passes* CHRISTIAN *and stops. Spots sign, picks it up to place on* CHRISTIAN *but stops.*

CHRISTIAN *is looking at him hopelessly.* NONDESCRIPT *turns sign around and hangs it on* CHRISTIAN *and walks off.* CHRISTIAN *looks at sign hanging on him which says in big letters, "HELP!" He looks out at audience dumbfounded and groans audibly.)*

(Blackout)

The TV Family

Purpose:

It is important for children to respect their parents. It is equally important for parents to live consistent lives that their children can respect. Sometimes arguments over things like what to watch on television make it difficult for a family member to act with respect, to have the kind of family relationship God intended. And if we can't even get along within our own families, how can we ever expect to show Christian love to the rest of the world?

Running time:

6-8 minutes

Cast:

DAD. Probably 40-50 years old. He's a football fan and likes to think of himself as the man in charge of the home, even though he doesn't completely understand the younger generation.

SON. Can be played anywhere from 10 to 14 years old. He's a bit of a smart aleck and has more of his father in him than either would care to admit. He usually speaks without thinking but somehow manages to say something intelligent now and then. Something that even surprises him!

Props:

1 folding chair to be used as Dad's favorite television chair

Application:

This sketch starts out quietly, slowly gathers momentum, and quickly builds without ever looking back! It is full of lines and reactions that an audience will instantly recognize and identify with. It is not unusual to see family members nudging each other as if to say, "That's just like you!" The simple thrust of the sketch deals with very real concerns of many families, yet the characters themselves should be played broadly, almost bigger than life. They actually serve as composite characters representing parts of everyone's parent or child.

The script itself offers a certain amount of leeway for characterization and staging. Both actors should take the time to develop the script's comic potential. The pantomime business involving the television will set the mood of the sketch right from the beginning. One word of warning: Don't let the somber message at the end of the sketch bog everything down. Don't be preachy or belabor the obvious message. The simpler the better. Just continue to act and react as a father and son might right through to the end.

This is one of those sketches that should speak for itself.

(A chair is directly center stage, imaginary TV set is played in front of chair a few steps.)

DAD *(enters, looking at his watch and yawning):* I think I'll watch a little TV here. *(Turns on set, steps back, folds his arms, waiting for the picture; looks offstage both directions to be sure no one is watching and suddenly steps forward and hits the side of the television.)* Ah, that's better . . . gotta know how to talk to 'em. Let's see here . . . *(flipping channels)* reruns, movie, football . . . football! Football is on TV, I can live again! *(Steps back to look at picture, suddenly jerks his head up and down, indicating the vertical hold isn't working.)* Wait a minute, here. Get ahold of that lousy vertical hold! *(Steps forward and adjusts knob. Still not pleased with the reception, he pulls up the imaginary rabbit ears antenna on top of the TV, tries to separate them, but they are evidently stuck. He gets his head momentarily caught between them. Jerks his head out and steps back muttering)* . . . That's fine, right there. *(Sits in chair.)* Don't pass on second down, you're gonna get killed . . . *(yawns)* fade back into the pocket . . . *(yawns)* . . . fade . . . fade . . . *(yawns)* . . . fade . . . back . . . into . . . the *(begins snoring deeply).*

SON *(enters, suddenly spots DAD sleeping, looks at TV, grimaces at the picture, tiptoes over to DAD, sticks his finger in DAD's ear to see how soundly asleep he is, then whispers):* Hey, Dad? *(DAD snores.)* You asleep? *(Another snore.)* I'm gonna change the channel, okay? *(DAD snores again.)* Thank you! *(Sits down in front of TV and switches channel.)* Oh, boy—a little Home Box Office, cable TV . . . *(Settles back and stares wide-eyed at television.)* The Spy Who Loved Me . . . *(Getting involved)* Look out, 007, the guy behind you. The guy, *(starts to yell)*

31

the guy behind you! *(Quickly covers his own mouth as* DAD *rustles, then settles back down to snoring.)* Look at that car, it has flippers. It's goin' in the water? How's it get traction? Watch out, there's a guy with a snorkel . . . *(Getting louder)* The guy with the snorkel, 007! *(Shutting himself up)* Put a lid on it. *(DAD is still deeply asleep.)* Oh, no! The spear gun, 007! Look out for the . . . *(Points at TV, yelling)* Look out behind you!

(What follows is chaos, DAD *jumping up looking behind him;* SON *jumping up, realizing he's awakened* DAD.)

DAD: What! What's behind me? What . . . *(He can't get a word in edgewise.)*

SON: Oh—oh! I didn't mean to wake you up. I'm sorry, I really am! I . . .

*(*SON *won't stop apologizing and* DAD *quickly raises his arm and makes a cutoff gesture.)*

DAD: Zip it! *(*SON *immediately shuts up and grins sheepishly.)* What happened to football? I was watching football on the TV.

SON *(innocently)*: Oh no, Dad. I came in here and you were sleeping.

DAD *(beat)*: I was resting my eyes. *(Arguing ensues.)*

SON: You were sleeping!

DAD: Don't argue with me. I know what I was doing. I was merely resting my eyes for a moment, that's all! I had that TV on the football game for a very good reason.

SON: You were sleeping! I could hear you in my bedroom, you sounded like a Sherman tank! So I changed the channel 'cause I wanted to watch a movie, *The Spy Who Loved Me.*

(After SON *announces the title of the movie,* DAD *abruptly stops. There is a moment of dead silence.)*

DAD: *The Spy Who Loved Me?*

SON *(quickly)*: I gotta watch it for an English class, Dad . . .

DAD: You mean, the James Bond movie with the girls in the bikinis and the machine guns.

SON *(knowing he's on thin ice)*: Well, that's the one, Dad.

DAD: Oh, noooo. Filthy, filthy, filthy! You are not going to watch that sex and violence on this TV! Trashy, trashy, trashy!

SON: There's nothing trashy about that movie. *(Idea hits him.)* Wait a minute, what about all the violence in football?

DAD (*after a moment of consideration*): Don't try to change the subject with me. We're talking about that movie, not football!

SON: Wait a minute! What about the Dallas Cowboy cheerleaders?

DAD (*knowing he's trapped*): Shut up. I'm your father and—

SON (*sensing a victory*): Aha! Double standards! You know what you are, you're a hypochrondriac!

DAD (*thinks, then attempts to correct him*): No, no. You mean I'm a hypocrite.

SON (*jumping at it*): Okay! You said it, not me.

DAD (*overlapping*): No! I didn't mean I was one, I was only helping you find the right word. If you'd go to school; get a vocabulary!

SON (*calming him down*): Dad, Dad. Sit down, rest your eyes. You work hard, you need to relax. Watch that blood pressure.

DAD (*mumbling*): You're the reason I got high blood pressure.

SON: I'm just gonna watch a little educational television. You're just a little too old-fashioned. (*Smiles soothingly, then sits back down in front of TV.*)

DAD (*those are fighting words; rises from chair and slowly builds*): Old-fashioned? Old-fashioned? Do you want to see how old-fashioned I can be? If that TV isn't turned off of that movie by the time I count to three, you are going to be one sorry boy . . . You hear me? One sorry boy! ONE . . . we're talking grounding. I'm not going to repeat myself, we're talking grounding . . . TWO . . . you are going to be in hot water, young man, hot water. (*Tries another tack.*) Your mother will be disappointed in you. THREE! (SON *has not flinched, he continues to stare at TV.*) That does it—you are grounded until you're 42!

SON (*rising*): That means I don't have to go to school anymore!

DAD: You know why I have to ground you?

SON: No; why?

DAD: Because you have no respect for your elders, that's why!

SON: Ah, Dad, I respect all you old p—— Oh-oh! (*Quickly covers his mouth, realizing he's committed another boo-boo.*)

DAD: You take that back! (SON *mimics the sound on a tape rewinding.*) That's not what I meant, and you know it!

SON: Well, how do you take something back! I don't—

DAD: Don't you sass me!

SON *(innocently)*: I'm not sassing you, Dad.

DAD: Watch your tone of voice!

SON *(speaks in lower tone of voice)*: I'm so sorry, Dad—

DAD *(incensed)*: I hate it when you do that!

SON: How do I know what you mean? I can't help it if my voice cracks; I'm at that age—

DAD: That's not what I meant and you know it! *(Raises his arms in finality.)* All right! Why should you listen to me?

SON *(quickly, without thinking)*: That's a good point. (DAD *glares at him.*) Just trying to be agreeable. *(Smiles weakly.)*

DAD: I mean, it's only scriptural that I'm head of the household. I mean, the TV was only purchased with money I worked so hard to earn. (DAD *steps forward, staring out over the TV gallantly.*) Why, I remember when I was a wee lad back during the big one! (SON *slaps his forehead as if "Here we go again."*) Why, I had to walk 15 miles in a blizzard just for a loaf of bread! We were so poor, I had one pair of shoes for all of us kids! Why, we were so poor—

DAD/SON: I didn't have a name until I was 12!

DAD: Oh, sure! What do you care? Selfish, selfish, selfish!

SON: I'm not selfish. I've just heard all these stories before.

DAD: No wonder you come home complaining about the fact that there was no love, no unity in your youth group at church!

SON *(interrupting him)*: That's not fair! Didn't you come home from work complaining that all you do is fight and bicker on the job? How are we ever gonna show love to the rest of the world if we can't get along here in our own family? *(He has spouted all this out without a breath.)*

DAD *(starts to argue, stops, starts again, then realizes his son has a point)*: Well, Son, maybe . . . maybe you've got a point.

SON *(beat)*: I do? What, what did I say?

DAD: Well, how can we ever expect to show love to the rest of the world if we can't even show it right here, in our own family? *(They look at each other.)*

(Slow fade)

The Beatitudes

Purpose:

Sometimes in the midst of all the difficulties we face in life, it is easy to forget that Jesus wants to be right there beside us to help us through any situation we might encounter. He knows how tough life can be sometimes. He's been through it all himself.

Running time:

5-6 minutes

Cast:

REPORTER *(Carries the bulk of this sketch himself.)*
SHOPPER
COWBOY
ASSERTIVE WOMAN
CHILD BRAT
CHRIST FIGURE

All the passersby may be played by only one actor or as many as five.

Props:

2 grocery bags which appear to be full
1 egg carton
1 10-gallon cowboy hat
1 huge, ugly purse (and wig, if played by male actor)
1 rubber ball
1 beanie or child-type cap

Application:

A quick glance at this script will show you that it is fully of activity. It is a physical piece with lots of action and broadly drawn characters. One of the primary concerns of the performance is timing, important for a couple of reasons. The timing and tempo of the delivery of lines should be sharp and crisp. The audience should sense lots of energy and momentum as the sketch moves from one character to the next. Also, each physical "schtick" should be bigger than the one before. Hence, the first character must start out small. The hit on the head with the egg carton is really nothing more than a "bop." You must leave room for the sketch to build and have someplace to go. Each character should sort of explode onto the stage, do what your character does, and disappear almost as quickly.

The reporter's job is to keep things moving, along with taking a beating. He should provide something for each character to bounce off of each time they appear. Another area of concern involving timing is the physical business of the sketch. This will probably seem obvious, but it is worth emphasizing. You will need to take the time to "choreograph" each hit, kick, or flip. Being familiar with each movement or action will accomplish a couple of things: It will insure a smooth, effective performance, and it will make sure no one ends up in traction!

The final moment of this sketch is another one of those surprise endings. It is not important for the Christ figure to appear or dress differently from the rest of the characters in the sketch. In fact, he should look just like the rest of us. Nor does His final gesture need to be theatrical or grandiose. The impact lies in the simple realization that He became like one of us so He understands our hurt, anger, frustration, joy, or sorrow. That final look between the reporter and the Christ figure should say it all.

❧ ❦ ❧

REPORTER (holding an imaginary microphone in his hand): Hi there, ladies and gentlemen! This is your tower of power, man of the hour, roving reporter. We're here in the streets of downtown ——— just asking innocent passersby their opinions of phrases from sacred literature. (HAGGARD SHOPPER crosses stage in front of REPORTER; arms loaded with grocery bags.) Ah! Excuse me . . . (Stops SHOPPER.) We're asking people their opinion of phrases from sacred literature, and we were wondering what you thought of the phrase "Blessed are the poor . . . , for they shall—"

SHOPPER (interrupting): Poor? Here, you want a dime? Get yourself a cup of coffee, just don't bug me. (Digs in pocket for dime.)

REPORTER: No, I don't want your dime; I want your opinion.

SHOPPER (*defensive*): My dime's not good enough for you, is that it?

REPORTER (*trying to placate* SHOPPER): No, I'm sure it is—

SHOPPER: Listen here, pal! A dime don't buy a nickel nowadays. Look at our economy! I'm so sick of hearing about all those people out of work. If all those people who weren't working would get jobs, there'd be no unemployment. Put that in your mouthwash and gargle with it.

REPORTER (*beat*): I'm sure there's wisdom somewhere in that statement, but what I—

SHOPPER (*pulls out carton of eggs*): You see these? $1.50! And they're not even jumbo! You've got some nerve, buddy, hasslin' me for my hard-earned money. Why don't you just get a job, you bum! (*Smacks him on the head with egg carton and swiftly exits.*)

REPORTER: Ouch! (*Calls after her.*) This *is* my job . . . (*Muttering*) Boy, kinda rough out here. (*Man with 10-gallon cowboy hat struts across, sees* REPORTER *and stops.*) Ah! Must be a native. Excuse me, sir, I was just asking people their opinion of certain phrases, and I was wondering if you'd offer your opinion.

COWBOY (*slapping* REPORTER *heartily on back,* COWBOY *stands bowlegged*): Okey-dokey! Shoot, I'm open, I'm open.

REPORTER: I was wondering what you thought of the phrase "Blessed are the merciful, for—"

COWBOY (*grabs* REPORTER *and puts him in a half nelson hold*): Mercy! Are you a draft dodger? Is that it, are you from Canada?

REPORTER (*struggling*): No, of course not—I didn't even vote for Goldwater!

COWBOY (*releasing him*): Good boy. I served my country, yes sirree! Korean War, 1939.

REPORTER (*correcting him*): Ah, 1952, I think.

COWBOY (*spinning around*): Are you questioning my word, boy?

REPORTER (*backpedaling*): No! Of course not; 1939 is fine.

COWBOY: I got wounded, too. (*Shows him his collarbone.*) See that, right there? (REPORTER *looks.*) I got hit with a spatula in the mess hall. Cook was mean! You want to talk about mercy, there was no mercy in my family. I was raised with 15 brothers and sisters. It was survival of the fittest in my home.

REPORTER: No kidding . . .

COWBOY: Take Sunday dinner, for instance. There we were, all around the table and I'd say to my sister Olga . . . Olga, she was ugly!

REPORTER: How ugly was she?

COWBOY: She was so ugly we put a CB on her and drove her as a truck. I'd say to Olga, I'd say, "How about passing me taters?" She'd say, "You want taters, I'll give you taters!" *(Hits* REPORTER *in stomach;* REPORTER *leans over in pain.)* She'd hit me just like that, and I'd run to the other side of the table! *(Goes to other side of* REPORTER.) I'd say to Jed—Jed, he wrestled with Olga—I'd say, "How about some butter?" He'd say, "You want butter, I'll give you butter." *(Karate chops* REPORTER *on back,* REPORTER *drops to knees.)* And he'd hit me just like that! *(*COWBOY *stops, realizing he's gotten carried away.)* Oh, I'm sorry. I plumb lost control of myself. *(Starts to help* REPORTER *up.)* Are you all right?

REPORTER: Yeah, I think so.

COWBOY *(dropping* REPORTER, *disgruntled):* Ahh, you wasn't listenin' to me anyway.

REPORTER: Yes, I was . . . I . . . *(gets to his feet).*

*(*WOMAN *enters and stops, as if waiting for bus. She carries a purse and looks very fragile.)*

REPORTER *(noticing her):* Ah, finally. A nice lady . . . *(Approaching her)* Excuse me, Miss—

WOMAN *(spins around and leaps into a karate pose and yells):* HiiYah!!

REPORTER *(jumping back):* I'm sorry! I was just wondering if you'd offer your opinion on a phrase from sacred literature?

WOMAN *(slowly relaxing):* I might . . .

REPORTER *(gently):* Wonderful. What do you think of the phrase "Blessed are the meek, for—"

WOMAN: Meek? Did you say meek? *(Walking up to him)* Did you know that 51 percent of this population is meek?

REPORTER: Well, no, I didn't.

WOMAN *(becoming agitated):* And do you know why we're meek? I'll tell you why we're meek. We're meek because we're supposed to be! You want to know what meek got me? Meek got me a hairful of rollers, a sinkful of dirty dishes *(throws out her arm gesturing for emphasis),*

38

and a husband who never comes home! *(Throws out other arm;* REPORTER *ducks to avoid being hit and crosses over to her other side.)*

REPORTER: Well, thank, you very much for your opinion, Miss—

WOMAN *(stunned):* Miss! *(Grabs his arm and flips him over her hip, he lands flat on the floor; she places one foot on top of him.)* Ms. to you, buster! *(Steps on over him and leaves.)*

REPORTER *(staggering to his feet):* Ms. it is . . . thanks for that . . . opinion . . .

*(*CHILD BRAT *comes on grinning widely, bouncing a ball, looking quite playful.)*

REPORTER: A nice child. I love kids; they say the cutest things. Excuse me?

CHILD BRAT *(scrunches up his face, sarcastically):* Whatta you want?

REPORTER *(beat):* I just met your mother—

CHILD BRAT: She ditched me in the supermarket, I think . . .

REPORTER: Could you give me your opinion on a phrase—

CHILD BRAT *(interrupting):* I'm not supposed to talk to strangers.

REPORTER: Well, I think it'll be okay this once.

CHILD BRAT *(grinning sheepishly):* Okay . . .

REPORTER: What do you think of the phrase "Blessed are the peacemakers, for—"

CHILD BRAT: Peacemakers? You ever try to be a peacemaker with *(holds up three fingers)* two older brothers? Well, it's not very easy! Like the other day, my brothers wanted to play football. You can't play football with *(holds up three fingers again)* just two people. So I said, "Okay guys, I'll be peacemaker. I'll play football with you."

REPORTER: That's nice.

CHILD BRAT: Yeah? Well, they didn't tell me I was going to be the football! And if you think I'm gonna make peace with you, you're crazy! *(Kicks him in the shin and starts to leave.)*

REPORTER *(hopping on one leg, holding his shin, sarcastic):* I just love little kids . . . (CHILD *comes back and kicks him in the other shin;* REPORTER *drops to floor as child exits.)* All right, that's it! *(At the end of his rope)* I don't have to take this! (MAN *enters and sees him, stops and listens.)* Nobody should have to put up with this kind of abuse! (REPORTER *sees* MAN, *very sarcastically speaks.)* Okay, one more try . . . *(Walks on his knees over to* MAN.) Excuse me, sir! *(angry)* What do you think of one phrase "Blessed are those who are persecuted *[gesturing to himself]* and reviled against and all manner of evil is said against them for *righteousness'* sake!!" *(Sticks microphone in* MAN's *face.)*

CHRIST FIGURE *(reaches out and helps* REPORTER *to his feet):* Why, yes. *(Touches the palms of his hands briefly, then holds them out to* REPORTER.) I know . . .

(Blackout)

He's Got My Number

Purpose:

The essence of our relationship with God is forgiveness. It is also essential to our relationships with each other. This sketch suggests that we sometimes let unimportant or trivial matters keep us from being able to forgive or seek forgiveness. It is vital that the reconciliation and restoration of relationships which forgiveness brings be evident in the lives of those who choose to follow Christ.

Running time:

9-11 minutes

Cast:

BOB. 30-50 years old, an average sort of guy. Somewhat pompous, he is amazed when someone questions his judgment on spiritual matters or cuisine.

FRANK. About the same age, very average sort of guy, inclined to play the martyr, especially when it is handy to do so.

Props:

4 folding chairs (*two for sitting and two for use as furniture*)
2 telephones (*one push-button; one rotary dial*)
2 Bibles (*one "New International Version" and one "Living Bible"*)
1 coupon in NIV Bible
1 chili-stained apron for BOB
1 chef hat for BOB (*paper type will do*)
1 feminine apron for FRANK
1 metal spatula for FRANK (*should be bent, twisted, mangled . . . you get the picture*)

Application:

This is one of our favorites! Probably because the dramatic style (simultaneous dialogue with unseen characters) is somewhat distinctive, and the message of forgiveness is an important one to consider. There are several areas where the actors should try to be sensitive in order to take full advantage of the script's potential. As we have said before, and will probably say again, the key to success is pacing and tempo. As one character's line is ending, the next line should be beginning. If line delivery overlaps some, so much the better. Both actors should decide on a fixed focal point at the back of the room that will serve as their wives for their conversation. It should go without saying that the actors should not acknowledge each other's presence. The audience must believe that even though these guys are just a few feet apart on the stage, the characters are really in their own living rooms carrying on conversations with their wives.

This is a script where the actors' job of painting word pictures is very important. Much of the sketch is spent describing previous events and the character's reaction to them. For the audience to get a sense of the importance of earlier events, the actors must be willing to show their characters reliving those moments of anger and humiliation. The facial responses, gestures, and movements of the characters must be vivid and full of energy. And while the characters must show evidence of anger or hurt pride, it is important not to let those emotions become so intense that they override the humor of the situation. The audience must like these two guys and be able to identify with them. We want the audience to laugh at themselves.

(*Two chairs stage left, two chairs stage right, one of each used as a stand on which rests a phone. Stage left side has a "New International Version" Bible leaning against the back leg of chair. Stage right side has "Living Bible" resting underneath push-button phone. Stage left phone is a disc dial type. Setting represents two almost identical homes.* BOB *enters stage left;* FRANK *enters stage right at same time.* FRANK *is wearing apron and carrying a twisted spatula.* BOB *is wearing chef hat which has a hole in it and an apron with a big chili stain on the front of it. Both march to their respective homes, open imaginary doors, enter, slam door, turn and look out at imaginary wife, and say:*)

BOB & FRANK (*almost together*): Honey, I'm home! How did the chili supper go? (FRANK *points to his spatula,* BOB *points to his apron stain.*) Does this answer your question?

BOB: Frank's chili!

FRANK: Bob's handiwork!

BOB: We could build the new educational wing of the church out of this stuff right here.

FRANK: Does this look like the spatula of a klutz who can't boil water? That's a direct quote. Bob called me a klutz in front of the entire church. *(Sits.)* And then he bent my spatula, my favorite spatula.

BOB: Then he covers me with his chili! If I hadn't grabbed that spatula out of his hand, who know what else he might have done. Hon, can you get the Pepto-Bismol? And looky here . . . *(Sticks his fingers through hole in his hat.)* He poofed my hat, my favorite hat.

FRANK: And all I did was spill a few drops of my chili on his apron—

FRANK & BOB: And he does this to me *(both pointing at their objects)*.

FRANK: This is the gratitude I get! Year after year I have volunteered to make that chili for the church supper. Why, everyone in the church loves my chili. *(Starts taking off his apron.)*

BOB: And you know how we have to put up with Frank's chili year after year. You should have seen everyone this year making a mad dash for the ice water.

FRANK *(folding apron):* Everyone was getting up for seconds of my chili, honey. Even the pastor made mention of it in his prayer.

BOB: You should have seen the pastor. He got up to pray and *(belches)* was all he could say!

FRANK: Hon, the pastor was stunned speechless. Well, you know that no one in that church holds a candle next to my chili.

BOB: We're lucky no one lit a match next to Frank's chili. The whole church could've gone up in flames. So I simply suggested in my own low-key, humble style that we might add a few tablespoons of water to his chili.

FRANK: Then he comes in with a garden hose to water down my chili. Well, that was the straw that broke the ol' proverbial camel's back. So I suggested that if he didn't want to eat my chili, then he could *wear* it! Then I picked up my bent spatula and slipped out the back of the church entirely unnoticed.

BOB: Then he makes this big scene, grabs his spatula, and storms out. And I'm left trying to scrape Frank's killer chili out before it eats through the bottom of the pan! If his kids have to eat that chili, it explains why they act the way they do. And when I think of all we've done for that family . . . How many times have we changed those kid's diapers while they've been off on vacation? Why, we have practically raised that family.

FRANK: When I stop to think of all the influence I've had over that family. . . . I've coached each one of their kids through Bible quizzing, each one dumber than the last. I'll never forget the time I asked the question, "Who wrote the Song of Solomon?" and little Bobby, Jr., pipes up with Bill Gaither.

BOB: Why, we have practically pampered them every day of their spiritual journey. When I stop to think of how many times we've had them over here and the four of us have spent hours sharing what the Lord has been doing in our lives . . . *(reflectively)* . . . Why, we've been through thick and thin together. (FRANK *glances at his phone—pause.*) Ha! He never hesitated to come over when we were having a barbecue, did he?

FRANK: He thinks my chili is bad, the last steak I had over at one of his barbecues was so rare it practically walked to my plate. I don't know where the tightwad gets his meat, but I know I heard that steak whinny before he threw it on the grille! And to think I looked up to this guy for spiritual guidance!

BOB: And when I think of what he did to me tonight . . . he's lucky he's not wearing that spatula for a hood ornament.

FRANK: To think one guy could get so upset over a little bowl of great chili. *(Rubs his stomach.)* Hon, get the Pepto . . .

BOB & FRANK *(both stare at wives)*: What? Call *him*? He's got *my* number!

BOB: That phone will be ringing any minute now; he knows I'm big enough to accept his apology.

FRANK: I'm bigger than this situation, Honey.

BOB: I'm not going to be petty about this. . . .

FRANK: I don't harbor any bitterness toward the guy. . . .

BOB: I'm not going to be vindictive about this. . . .

FRANK: My motto is forgive and forget. . . .

BOB & FRANK: Maybe . . . *(both look at phones)* . . .

BOB: Somebody's got to make the first move.

FRANK *(looking up)*: What?

BOB (*looking up*): You don't mean me?

FRANK: I could if I wanted. Oh, yes, I could . . . Oh, yeah! Double dare? All right, I will. (*Slowly wilts.*) You mean . . . now?

BOB (*sits and begins dialing on disk phone*): Hon, this may not be a pretty sight.

FRANK: You might want to leave the room, Honey. (*Sits and punches number on push-button phone. Both finish at same time.*)

BOB & FRANK: Busy! (*Both hang up and cross arms simultaneously.*)

BOB: I can just imagine the rumors he's spreading about me right now over that phone. How many times have I gone the second mile for that guy. All I ever do is give, give, give.

FRANK: Take, take, take . . . that's all that guy every did. Give him an inch, he always took a mile. I can just imagine the stories he's broadcasting about me right now. (*Gets an idea.*) I'm gonna be ready for him. I'm gonna load up on scripture to nail him with Sunday! (*Gets up looking for Bible.*) Hon, have you seen my Bible? (*Stops and stares at her.*) Of course I know what it looks like; don't get smart. (*Finds it under the phone.*) Here it is, right where I always keep it. (*Sits and blows off dust.*)

BOB: You can just bet he's loading up with ammo to blast me out of the water on Sunday. Well, I'm gonna have a comeback for every one of his potshots! Oh, yeah, I can back it up with scripture. You seen my Bible? What do you mean, it's right where I left it when I read the kids the Christmas story? Do you realize how long ago . . . never mind, I'll find it myself. (*He finds it and sits; both of them are thumbing through.* FRANK *is closing his eyes, opening the Bible, and letting his finger fall, checking, and then trying again. They both find the verse. They tap it knowingly and speak.*)

BOB & FRANK : Aha! "Vengeance is mine, saith the Lord"! (See Ps. 94:1.)

FRANK: Let him refute that! (*Thumbs some more.*)

BOB (*continuing to read the same verse*): O Lord, . . . shine forth. Rise up, O Judge of the earth; pay back to the proud what they deserve. . . . But the Lord . . . will repay them . . . and destroy them for their wickedness; the Lord our God will destroy them" (Ps. 94:1-2, 22-23, NIV).

FRANK (*finding another one*): "It is hard to stop a quarrel once it starts, so don't let it begin (*A little shocked . . .*) Love forgets mistakes; nagging about them parts the best of friends" (Prov. 17:14, 9, TLB). (*He stares,*

taken back by what he has read. Beat, then) Oooh, I don't want that.
(Starts thumbing.)

BOB *(mumbling)*: Where's all that mean stuff? There's gotta be some mean
stuff.

FRANK *(mumbling)*: What about Paul? Paul had something to say about
everything. *(Starts thumbing again.)* Book of Paul . . . Book of Paul . . .
(Can't seem to locate it.) Must be Old Testament.

BOB *(finding one)*: "Judge not, lest ye be judged! . . . Why do you look at
the speck of sawdust in your brother's eye and pay no attention to
the plank in your own eye? How can you say to your brother, 'Let
me take the speck out of your eye,' when all the time there is a plank
in your own eye? You hypocrite . . ." (see Matt. 7:1, 3-5, NIV).

FRANK: "Don't criticize, and then you won't be criticized. For others will
treat you as you treat them" (Matt. 7:1-2, TLB).

BOB & FRANK *(both thoughtfully pause, look up—then)*: Naaa! There's gotta
be somethin' better in here . . .

FRANK *(mumbling)*: What's all this red print?

BOB *(finds something)*: An old McDonald's coupon—1967. Probably not
any good.

FRANK: Book of Collisions; what's that?

BOB *(reading)*: "You, my brothers, were called to be free. . . . serve one
another in love. . . . 'Love your neighbor as yourself.'" Well, who hid
little Frankie, Jr.'s, pet birthday hamster for two weeks before his
birthday! Maybe the clothes dryer wasn't the best place, but still . . .
(Continues reading.) "If you keep on biting and devouring each other,
watch out or you will be destroyed by each other" (Gal. 5:13-15,
NIV).

FRANK: "Since you have been chosen by God . . . you should practice
tenderhearted mercy and kindness to others" (Col. 3:12). Who
played Santa Claus for his kids when he was down with the flu
New Year's Eve! I'd do anything for—*New Year's* Eve! No wonder he
was upset! *(Looks at phone.)*

BOB: "For the fruit of the Spirit is love, joy, peace, patience, kindness,
goodness, faithfulness, gentleness and self-control" (Gal. 5:22-23,
NIV).

FRANK: "Be gentle and ready to forgive; never hold grudges. Remember,
the Lord forgave you, so you must forgive others" (Col. 3:13). *(He*

puts Bible down and picks up bent spatula, stares at it, then) Maybe I'm not the Galloping Gourmet . . . *(dials the phone).*

BOB *(touches his chili stain and tastes it):* I guess his chili isn't that bad.

FRANK (humming to himself): Reach out, reach out and touch someone . . .

BOB *(answering phone):* Hello. . . . Frank?

FRANK: Yeah, listen, Bob, I just wanted to call and say I'm sorry about what happened.

BOB: Me too.

FRANK: You know that stain on your apron?

BOB: Yeah, it's right here.

FRANK: You soak that in a little kerosene and V-8 juice, it'll come right out of there.

BOB: Really? Well, you take a blowtorch and vise grip to that spatula, it'll be as good as new.

FRANK: Don't worry about it, everything is going Rubbermaid, anyway. Hey! I've got a little leftover chili. Why don't you herd the family into the Buick and come on over ? (BOB *stares at the phone.)* Hello?

BOB: Sure, why not. I think I've gotta couple steaks in the deep freeze, I'll throw 'em in, too.

FRANK *(quickly clutching at straws):* Ahhh, our microwave's on the blink.

BOB: I can thaw 'em over here!

FRANK *(with a grimace):* Well, praise the Lord . . . I'll catch you in a while.

BOB: Right. Bye!

BOB & FRANK *(both hang up and stare forward):* Oh-oh. Honey! Better get the Pepto!

(Blackout)

Moments
(A Monologue)

Purpose:

By exploring our relationship with our parents we may learn more about our relationship with our Heavenly Father. Sometimes in the crises of life we discover the importance of our relationship with God.

Running time:

10-11 minutes

Cast:

One man 20-40 years old

Props:

Piece of a jigsaw puzzle

Application:

This piece is a parallel spiritual journey and family relationship. It should be recounted simply and with feeling. You should be prepared to be emotionally involved and vulnerable to bring this character to life. The monologue should move quickly, especially in the early stages. But never be afraid to take the time to let the audience feel the warm moments or the intensity of the conflict.

The final moment should be one of feeling, but not too heavy-handed or overemotional. Let the simplicity of the script work for you.

When people believe the character, they will share in the understanding of its message.

(Discovers a piece of a jigsaw puzzle): A piece of a jigsaw puzzle. Somewhere someone has a picture of a mountain range with a peak missing! Or the signing of the Declaration of Independence without Thomas Jefferson! I haven't seen one of these in a long time. That's funny too. Because I kind of grew up with puzzles.

I can still remember Dad hunched over the card table in the living room trying to piece together a puzzle of a New England coastline. Mount Rushmore, or some faraway exotic place. He almost always got one for Christmas. He would spend hours working on it. Sometimes he would glue all the pieces together and frame the picture. We kids would all applaud and Mom would file the picture with the rest in the back of the hall closet.

Momma always said that working puzzles helped relax him. Maybe it was supposed to. But I could never resist sneaking into the living room, reaching up on the table when I thought he wasn't looking, stealing a piece of the puzzle, and making a mad dash to escape unnoticed!

I would wait impatiently just around the corner, clutching my valuable treasure. Pretty soon, the puzzle would be complete except for my piece. Dad would act surprised and call out, "I can't find the last piece of the puzzle. The most important piece of the puzzle is missing!"

I would hardly wait for him to finish before I would go running into the room, laughing gleefully, waving the missing piece of puzzle in my hand. He was never angry or impatient. He would grab me up onto his lap and chuckle as I proudly took the last piece of the puzzle and pushed it into place.

He would always tell me I was the most important piece to him. The picture wasn't complete without me. I guess like any other kid my age I couldn't imagine a safer place in the whole world than my father's lap with his arms around me.

I suppose I was different in some ways from most kids. I grew up in the church. I was kind of a professional religious person. We were always the last ones to leave church on Sunday mornings. I was playing shepherds in Christmas pageants almost before I could talk! I'll never forget the time my mother put my King Herod beard on with airplane glue! For a week I was the only third grader at school who looked like he was 45 years old.

Mom and Dad believed in being involved in the church. They also believed in things like prayer, not to mention God's will and acting spiritual. I guess as I was growing up, I never realized how important all that was to my parents. They centered their lives around God.

Oh, sometimes I got a little tired of it all. But I kind of liked the secure feeling church gave me. I was content for my parents to look out for me and take care of me. At least I was until I got a little older. I didn't mind going to church that much. It was just that there were other things I wanted to do. My family didn't seem to realize that you can only take so much of one thing.

My brother and sister didn't help the situation much. They were always winning something or other. And no matter how hard they tried, they were always well liked. I don't think Mom and Dad thought they could do anything wrong. I tried to be like them. But I just couldn't get that enthused over Sunday School contests, piano lessons, or good grades.

Soon my brother and sister started leaving for college. Dad worked more than ever. We didn't spend much time together. I hardly ever saw him working a puzzle anymore.

The time we spent together was usually limited to discussing the earthshaking issues of adolescence. Like most kids I was convinced that my parents had never been my age in their lives. So I treated them accordingly. They tried to use words like *groovy* and *neat*, but it wasn't the same. So between their work and my friends and school we didn't spend much time together.

I didn't spend that much time at church either. Maybe Mom and Dad thought I would automatically follow in their footsteps. But, after all, there were things I wanted to do.

I had some big plans for my life. There were so many things I thought I wanted to do and be. But I guess most of my friends weren't filled with the same lofty aspirations. It got to be a lot easier to settle for "good times" and relationships that demanded very little of me. Integrity and discipline kind of took a back seat. It got a lot easier to be motivated by prestige, recognition, or money. Now you see, my friends weren't all dopers or completely without morals. There wasn't much depth to their lives. I mean I don't know what they were really living for.

Well, I guess all those jigsaw puzzles kind of gave me an eye for color and symmetry. It seemed like I could draw or illustrate just about anything. I had a lot of other interests. But I had always been intrigued by artists, writers, photographers. I hadn't given much thought to it, but I kind of thought I might like to do something like that someday. Besides, it was something that nobody in my family was interested in or able to do but me.

About this time, my friends and I got a great idea. Why not just take off and travel around the country, maybe even Europe? We thought it would be a great way to experience life. And forget school and other hassles. I told Mom and Dad that it was the kind of thing people like Hemingway did when they were young.

Mom and Dad weren't too sure about how great the opportunity was. Something about maturity and discipline. So they decided it would be wiser if we waited until I was older. They didn't seem to think it was such a big deal.

Well, I couldn't believe it! I was sure this was my big chance to get out and discover who I really was. It was my big career opportunity. I could practically see my own mansion with a Mercedes parked in front of it! Maybe we all have moments in our lives that we are positive are turning points. For me, it seemed like a quest for independence.

Suddenly it seemed like all my life my parents had been trying to keep me from doing what I wanted to do. This was my chance to prove to them that I was something special. And they seemed to be trying at every turn to make me into somebody I didn't want to be.

I remember storming into the living room where Mom and Dad were sitting.

"You don't understand me, do you?" I blurted out.

Surprised, they both looked up as Dad started to respond. But I wasn't listening.

"You're ruining my one chance for success. You don't even care about what I want to do!"

Dad smiled a little tiredly. "Sure I do. It's just that we prayed about it and thought it would be best if—"

"What's best? How do you know what's best for me or anybody? You've wasted your whole life at a lousy job and putting puzzles together. What have you got to show for it?"

I saw a look of hurt pass through his eyes. It wasn't like any look I had seen before. But words full of anger and frustration kept tumbling out. And I knew I couldn't call them back.

"I'm going to make something out of my life. And I don't need you. I'm sick of your straight and narrow life. I'm sick of you. I'm sick of those endless puzzles!"

It would have been nice if I could have made some dramatic exit and left home. But I didn't. I guess I might as well have. I waited until I finished school. One day while Mom and Dad were at work I wrote them a note saying good-bye and left.

I never knew why, why any of it happened. It made no sense. All I knew was that I felt a little lost and empty. Not my "freedom" or anything I had wanted was worth it.

Well, I got a job kind of doing what I wanted. I guess I did all right. Wherever I was in my travels I would always drop Mom and Dad a card at Christmas filled with meaningless news. They would always send back letters full of family chatter and themselves. But it wasn't the same. Sure, there were times when I wanted to go back . . . but, somehow, I couldn't.

At least, not until the other day when I got a call from home. It could have been one of those melodramatic scenes from a movie or TV show. The kind of thing that always happened to someone else. My sister wasn't supposed to be telling me that it was my father who had been rushed to the hospital.

I walked into a dimly lit hospital room to see my father lying there. My mother was sitting by the bed clutching his hand. She looked at me, smiling weakly, tears filling her eyes. I stood at the end of the bed staring at my father.

Suddenly, I saw three kids slowly tiptoeing into our parents' bedroom. Then peering intently at their sleeping forms over the foot of the bed. Soon enough our whispers would wake Mom, who would motion for us to be quiet. But our anticipation of what lay downstairs on a Christmas morning was hard to contain. Our giggled responses were usually enough to arouse Dad. He would offer a groggy ho-ho-ho and we would all troupe downstairs. I will never forget how he seemed so wise and peaceful sleeping there. Yet I knew that when he woke up and we journeyed forth to make our discoveries, he would always know exactly what I wanted or needed. Those were moments when I couldn't even imagine what my life would be like without my dad in it.

After I left home and my family, my friends used to say, "So what about you and your dad. That's the way it is in a lot of families today. We all have to live our own lives. What's so important about you and your father sharing your lives?"

But when I saw my father lying there . . . it was important.

I bent over the side of the bed and gathered my arms around him.

"I'm sorry," I whispered, "I never meant to hurt you. I just wanted you to . . ."

He didn't hear me. Suddenly I knew he never would.

And for some reason I thought of all those times when I was young, when I would come running in with that important missing piece of puzzle. And he was always there to take me up and surround me with his arms. He would always tell me that God loved me and thought I was important too. He said that God would always be a little sad as long as I was missing. And my life would always feel a little empty.

There, holding my father, I felt how incomplete my life had been without his love in it. And I knew how sad I must have made him.

I think I know now how He must feel. During all my struggles to give my life worth and meaning, He was right there with His arms held open, waiting for me to bring the most important piece of the puzzle to Him. Maybe it's time to give it up and let Him put it all together.

"If you're still missing a piece, I just want to say . . . I'm sorry. I never meant to leave You. But I'm here now. I'm here."

A Man Out of Time: A Personal Confession
(A Monologue)

Purpose:

Saying we are Christians is not enough. Our life-style must say it louder than our words. And it is a change that occurs from the inside out. At one time or another we each confront Jesus Christ and choose either to follow or turn away. And even if we choose to not choose, in doing so, we are actually choosing.

Once, long ago, Someone chose to die for us. That is a fact we cannot deny. And how we reconcile His death in our own lives makes for eternal implications.

Running time:

7-8 minutes

Cast:

Jesus. A man of average age, 20-40 years old

Props:

None

Application:

This piece can be performed either as an oral interpretation or a memorized dramatic monologue. The character begins his story simply and objectively. But as he continues to tell it, he becomes progressively caught up in it. Until, in the end, he is a man haunted by his personal confrontation with Jesus Christ, a confrontation which we, the audience, realize he will never be able to forget.

Stage movement and interpretation have been left to the discretion of the performer. The piece should run approximately 7-8 minutes, no longer. Pace is important and the piece should continue to build with the intensity through the Crucifixion. There is a definite mood shift from the beginning to the end. What begins for the character as a simple, objective account of events becomes a very personal confession and ends on a very somber, reflective note.

They named me Jesus. I don't know why, I guess my mother just liked the name, and my father . . . well, he didn't seem to care much. There's nothing wrong with the name in itself; that's a good name, Jesus. Wait a minute, don't get me wrong. I'm not *the* Jesus. But the name wasn't that uncommon and there were many of us given the name of Jesus by our parents. I just happened to be one of the Jesuses at the same time the *real* Jesus was living too. In fact, we were pretty close to the same age, I think. Now don't misunderstand me, I never really knew the Man or all that He believed in. But I did meet Him once.

I think I saw Him once as a child, too. I can remember the scene vividly. My father and I were passing through a small village on our way to visit relatives, and there were a whole bunch of kids my own age playing on the mudbank of a stream. They were all wildly flinging mud everywhere, at the houses and innocent passersby, of which I happened to be one. And as we went on by them I heard someone yell out, "Hey, Jesus!" Well, I turned around to see who was yelling at me, and I saw this tall, lanky kid throw a mudball at someone else . . . someone else. He threw it at a boy who was on His hands and knees huddled over a mound of clay. The Boy jerked His head to one side as the mudball flew on past Him. And He looked up and laughed at His friend's poor aim. The lanky kid chuckled too and turned back to his other buddies. But this Boy turned back to concentrate on His own creation. Somehow, that Kid my own age was different. Now, there He was, mud caked on His face, matted in His hair, all over His clothes! Almost oblivious, it seemed, to the rest of them who were joyfully flinging mud everywhere, with the innocence and abandonment only children seem to possess. I can remember the contrast of that scene. It struck me then as a child and still comes to mind now. There was this *other* Jesus, right in the middle of all that blissful chaos . . . and yet, so apart and intent on accomplishing His own purpose.

Well, who knows . . . it probably wasn't even the same Jesus that I heard so much about as I grew up. But every now and then I'd hear stories or rumors about some Man named Jesus and the miraculous things He'd done or something profound that He had said. He said a lot . . . *He* said He was the Messiah, my mother said He was of God, and my father said He was of the devil. And I . . . well, I didn't say much of anything. After all, this Man was using my name. It wasn't hurting my own reputation . . . in fact, quite the opposite. Oh, sure, people who knew me would tease me and ask me to turn their water into wine. And we'd all laugh and chuckle at the thought. . . . But those people who didn't know me, strangers who would just be passing through our town, once they heard my name, they treated me differently than the ordinary person. I became someone *special*. Well, I didn't mind playing the part. As long as they didn't find out who I really was. In fact, it came too easily. People would ask me to bless their crops or their business, or heal some illness, and . . . I didn't see any harm in turning my Namesake into a little popularity for myself. After all, He was using my name just as much as I was using His. And aren't we all willing to be identified with a cause or a figure if we think it's going to boost our own image in the eyes of others? Well, so was I. . . . until I happened to meet Him.

It was on a hillside. There was a multitude of people and one by one they'd just go up to Him and He'd bless them, or touch them, or just talk to them. Why not? I thought. So I casually mingled among the crowd until I saw He had a spare moment, and I went up to Him and I grabbed His hand. His hand felt just like anybody else's. "My name's Jesus, too." He didn't say anything. He just kept that steady gaze on me. "Of course, I'm not anything like You."

He slowly smiled, and then He said, "No, not on the inside."

"No. Not on the inside but I've got Your name, haven't I? We, we have the same name . . ." He didn't say anything else. He just kept that steady gaze on me as I . . . I stumbled backwards and . . . got myself lost in the crowd. That was the only time we ever met . . . but I've never forgotten it. (*Wondering what He meant: "Not on the inside."*)

Anyway, after that incident I just quit blessing people's crops and told them I wasn't the Man . . . the Man they thought I was. That was several years ago, I don't know why I thought of it now.

I saw Him one other time, about half a year ago. Again it was on a hillside, only He wasn't healing or speaking or touching; He was dying. I don't know, I guess things went bad for Him. You see, I never listened to the rumors or the neighborhood gossip. Although I did understand that a few people gave up everything just to be with Him . . . I wonder what they're doing now? Anyway, it was a bad one.

It wasn't your typical crucifixion. People were shoving and pushing on all sides just to get closer to this Man . . . just to watch Him stumble up a hill with His death tree. People were running up to Him and throwing sand in His face and grinding gravel into the raw muscles of His back where He'd been whipped. And as He went on by me, I saw His face . . . You see, His eyes were swollen shut and His cheeks were puffed up from being slapped so many times. And His hair and beard were literally hanging in strands from His face where people had run by and jerked and yanked on it until they'd ripped it from the flesh by the roots . . . And as they nailed flesh to wood, mothers huddled their children about them and turned their faces inwards. I watched them raise the tree and . . . and I winced as His hands tore when the soldiers dropped the cross into a hole they had dug to brace it up. And yet . . . as I stared up at His face . . . I couldn't help but see a child toiling over a mound of mud again. No, there was no longer *mud* caked on His face, but there He was again. Right in the middle of a mob that was jeering, spitting, and cursing His name into oblivion. Yet, His face remained intent on accomplishing some purpose.

I didn't stay around any longer. I imagine He died rather slowly, but I didn't care to watch . . . I'd seen enough. I don't know why I keep thinking about it. I hadn't until a couple weeks ago. I was going through town to get some fresh water and I heard someone behind me yelling, "Jesus! Jesus!" Instinctively, I turned around to see a . . . a small boy running towards me. And the instant my eyes met his, he suddenly stopped. He stared up at me . . . he looked terribly confused and bewildered. "Are, are you Jesus?" For a moment I thought I felt the gaze of a man on a hill, full of power and love. And I had to tell him, "No . . . no, I'm *not* Jesus . . . not on the inside." For some reason that question haunts me. But I'll get over this feeling . . . *(looking lost)* I always do . . .

(Slow Fade)